DARPAN

ONE

STEP

CLOSER

to death.

Contents

*To all the right people
in the wrong place —you'll find
your home soon.*

ACKNOWLEDMENTS

I owe a huge thank you to my parents and siblings first—your unshakable belief in my dreams and your endless love have always been my foundation and strength. Every word I write is filled with the warmth of your support. Thank you for helping me bring my words to the world.

To my forever seven —Namjoon, Seokjinie, Yoongi, Hobi, Jimin, Taehyung and Jungkook— your music and messages have been a soundtrack to my writing sessions and a beacon during my moments of doubt. Thank you for teaching me the power of passion and perseverance. Saying thank you is an understatement because I am very grateful to you. Thank you for being our purple whale.

Tay—thank you for showing me that even with a broken heart, I can create. If Taylor Swift can rise above despite the hate and pain, then so can I.

To my best friend, Megha—you know who you are and how deeply I value you. You've been my sounding board, my midnight call, and my laughter in the dark. Love how this book had not just me but even you working overtime. Thank you for pushing me to write and publish — this book is as much yours as it is mine.

To all my friends—Vanshika, Yachna, Shrishti, Yashaswi, Aastha, Rashi—and those not named, thank you for standing by me. Your encouragement and honest critiques have been invaluable. I am blessed to have each of you in my life.

This book carries a piece of each of you, and for that, I am eternally grateful. Thank you for being part of my journey.

And lastly thank you notion press publishing for giving me a chance to make my dream come true.

Forever grateful,

Darpan.

PLAYLIST

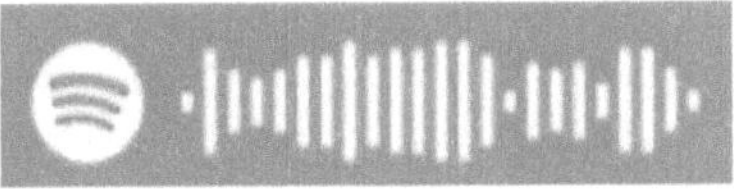

Family Line — Conan Gray

Older — Sasha Alex Sloan

Nothing New — Taylor Swift, Phoebe Bridgers

Matilda — Harry Styles

Fine Line — Harry Styles

The Cut That Always Bleeds — Conan Gray

Stay Alive — Jung Kook (Prod. SUGA of BTS)

Tolerate it — Taylor Swift

Chemtrails Over the Country Club — Lana Del Rey

The Archer — Taylor Swift

Would've Could've Should've — Taylor Swift

Too Sad to Cry — Sasha Alex Sloan

I Miss You, I'm Sorry — Gracie Abrams

Sweet Nothing — Taylor Swift

Film Out — BTS

Hoax — Taylor Swift

Blue & Grey — BTS

Haunted (Taylor's Version) — Taylor Swift

My Tears Ricochet — Taylor Swift

This Is Me Trying — Taylor Swift

The Great War — Taylor Swift

For Us — V

Shot Glass of Tears — Jung Kook

Snow On the Beach — Taylor Swift, Lana Del Rey

Who's Afraid of Little Old Me — Taylor Swift

I can do it with a broken heart —-Taylor Swift

You won't remember

all my

CHAMPAGNE PROBLEMS

ONE STEP CLOSER

Please, look at me.

You see my tears,
They're there, clear as day.
But you,
you're somewhere else,
Even when you're right here.

You know what makes me smile,
Those little nothings,
Yet,
it's like you're fading,
Fading away in quiet.

Am I a bad child?
Or is it just,
Just that to you,
I'm like air,
There but not really there.

My mother,

You knew me before I knew anything.
But now,
It's like you don't see me,
Just see through me.

People ask you,
'How's your kid?'
And you,
you just smile,
But why stop there?
Why not really know me?

Here I am,
Under the same big sky,
Wishing you'd really see me.
Not just with your eyes,
But see all of me,
The real me,
Not just skin and bones,
But the soul inside,
Just me.

DARPAN

Nothing has changed, then why won't you?

5

I wish you knew,
under all this pain,
there's love still.
Big, like the sky
after a storm.

Remember when?
Life was just
Saturday cartoons
and your laugh,
so easy.

Now, I've grown.
Words about you
are like glass,
sharp in my throat.

Those days,
I was just a kid,

you were just my dad,
easy, like Sunday mornings.

I wish we could go back,
to when I didn't see
the hard edges of the world.
Just you and me,
and everything simple.

But here we are,
you and me,
and all this space
in between.
I still love you, Papa.

Still,
I love you,
that never changed,
through the storms,
through the estranged.

If I had to choose,
your life or mine,
without a pause,
yours
...every time.

In the quiet, in the strife,
my love for you, as big as the sky.
Wish you could see that,
through all this grown-up mess,
that I am today.

ONE STEP CLOSER

Why do you leave... and not see me at all?

You told me once,
so gently,
"I never let you cry when you were small."
But now, my tears,
they just fall and fall,
and I'm here wondering,
why does my heart feel so raw?

You used to call me precious,
but what's different now?
Why does it feel like
you're breaking me,
over and over,
and I'm left craving for light,
somehow?

In my heart,
my love for you is still alive,
but it's like you're blind,

blind to how much I care.
And I'm here asking myself,
am I worth your fight,
or am I just air?

My eyes, they caught a sight,
a father and daughter,
so full of life, so tight.
Their laughter, it echoed,
and filled me with a bitter night,
'cause it reminded me,
of what we're not,
not quite.

Did I earn this,
this cold fate?
To feel alone,
this bad?
In my sadness, I sit and wait,
thinking,
why can't things be like before?

Once, you were my sunlight,
bright and sure,
now there's just shadows,
where love once was pure.
I'm wandering alone, no end in sight,
Where's the joy
where's the light?

So I write these lines,
heavy and slow,
hoping they find you,
even if you don't show.
I promise, I'm trying to grow,
finding my peace,
where only sadness used to flow.

You told me once,
"No more tears in your eyes,"
but now they fall,
unending like the skies.

And as I cry,
I keep asking,
why,
why you left,
breaking our once perfect ties.

ONE STEP CLOSER

*Why am I left with only myself to wound up
more?*

They say, I'm who I should be,

The grown-up version of a kid's dream,

But when I look in the mirror,

I'm not so sure,

it's not what it seems.

I think of me, way back when,

Running wild, free, and bold,

Now I'm here, all grown up,

Am I what she hoped,

in the stories told?

What if I scare her, the younger me,

With my grown-up ways,

my tired eyes?

Did I lose the dreams she had,

Underneath these adult skies?

What if I look at her

and all I want is to hold too tight,

to stop her laughter,

her dreams,

to strangle the air, she breathes?

And sometimes I think,

in the quiet,

What if I could erase now,

to disappear,

to go back to what was?

Am I the monster, in her closet?

The shadow, in her night?

Or the grown-up

she didn't want to be,

When she was young, and full of light?

But, no what ifs and buts,

can change,

That She's in me,

still, that little girl,
With her dreams, her laugh, her spark,
I'm her —grown up, yes, but still,
We're both here, in the light and the dark.

DARPAN

Can't you see me in a way which doesn't
give me bruises?

I look across the room, there you are, Mom,

Your eyes land on me,

But it's like you don't really see.

You look, but there's this coldness,

Like you're looking right through me.

You're amazing,

everyone says,

But those eyes, they're just...

empty,

When they rest on me.

It's like you hate me,

Not for something I did,

But because I remind you of you.

You're scared I'll end up like you,

That's why you can't stand me, isn't it?

I look back at you,
and I get it,
I really do.
This weird dislike, not for who you are,
but because I see too much of you in me,
and it bothers me too.

You say I'm too much like you,
and it's not a compliment.
I hear that.
I can't stand that,
not because you're wrong,
but because you had to say it.

It bugs me,
the way you see me,
but more than that,
I wish you hadn't brought me into this world
just to be a mirror for you.

DARPAN

Just for once, hear me out.

I scribble lines,
poems, my heart in words,
But you, Mother,
your eyes elsewhere,
on them, not me.

"Look, listen, these words, they're mine,"
my words, a whisper,
lost in the air,
You, already sailing,
on a different sea.

You promise, "I'll hear you,"
but the words are empty,
like rain clouds that never pour.
You're caught up,
in stories, that are not mine.

They talk, you smile,

their day, their dreams,
Me? Invisible,
standing, silent.

I try and try, "Ma, listen,"
but it's like echoes in a canyon,
You're there, but not for me,
Your attention, a gift,
not mine to receive.

You, my world,
but to you, I'm just a shadow, fading,
in their bright light.

It stings, yeah,
your silence to me, a scream,
I'm here with you,
but are you?

Useless. A good for nothing, you say,
Me, with a heart full of dreams,

DARPAN

Can I really smile,

when you see me as a mistake?

How can I be,

when to you, I'm nothing,

just a blank page,

in your book full of stories.

How do I keep going,

when you don't see me?

When even your gaze,

says I'm nothing,

nothing in front of their perfections.

How to be,

when even you,

don't see me,
    really see me.

ONE STEP CLOSER

I tell you, please, close the door,

you say you always do.

But no, you don't.

It's clear to me,

you never do.

Even though I've told you,

it makes me feel so small.

You shrug it off,

"It's not that big,"

but do you see me at all?

When it's open,

I can't help but stare,

making sure there's nobody there.

Nobody watching me.

But the moment I look away,

it feels like it's always there—

watching,
until I look back,
and then there's nobody.

"You're just being paranoid,"
you say,
I know.
But I also know that you won't change,
won't close the door.
But I will.

I will close the door
of my heart to you.
Because you can't see,
or won't see,
what leaving it open does to me.

ONE STEP CLOSER

You ruined it, but can't you try to fix it?

Our house
where whispers turn to shouts
I stand small, unseen
between walls
that echo fights
not of my making
but of my living.

My heart, a sponge
absorbing tears and screams,
silent witness to the crumbling
of what I thought was my rock
my home, my haven
now just a battleground
for those who once whispered
love in my sleepy ears.

In the garden of my youth
where innocence bloomed,

petals fall, one by one
withered by the frost of anger,
the drought of affection,
I learned too soon
the language of sorrow, the dialect of loss.

Eyes wide open,
to the imperfections of those
who were my giants
heroes in my storybooks
now just humans flawed, fractured
fighting battles
I wish I could mend.

The invisible scars,
carve lessons into my soul
trust becomes a bridge
too fragile to walk on
love, a concept
tainted by conditions
I grow old in the heart

while still young in years.

My voice, a whisper
lost in the cacophony of their war.
I learn
to speak in silences,
to find solace in the solitude,
my companions
the shadows of what was.

The innocence of childhood,
a delicate vase shattered on the floor
of reality
I pick up the pieces
not to restore
but to remember
the beauty it once held
before the fall.

Now, I walk, a ghost among memories
learning to rebuild

not the innocence lost

but the strength found in the ruins

of a childhood

that witnessed too much

too soon.

ONE STEP CLOSER

You don't try at all, it's like you don't want
me.

We're in the same room
But it feels like miles apart.
I say "hey,"
You nod,
That's it.

I came from you,
Isn't that supposed to mean something more?
We talk, but it's like
Echoes in a big, empty space.

I look at you,
Wishing we could laugh,
Share secrets, or just sit and be,
But it's like we're on different pages
Of a book that was never opened.

I want to tell you everything,

But the words get stuck.
You ask how I'm doing,
"I'm fine," I say.
But inside, I'm shouting,
"Can't you tell I'm not?"

Could have been,
should have been—
those thoughts haunt me.
We're like two ships,
passing too far in the night
to even wave.

I just want a sign,
something to show
that you feel this gap too,
that you wish, like I do,
for a bridge
to cross over to each other.

But it's hard,

Like there's a glass wall between us.
You can see through,
But can't touch,
Can't really connect.
I whisper, "I miss you,"
to the space where the words
get lost.

Every day, I hope,
Maybe today we'll break the glass,
Start to really talk,
Really listen,
Really connect.

But days turn to nights,
And we stay on our sides,
Close enough to touch,
Yet worlds apart.

I wanted us to be a story
of laughter,

of shared secrets,
of hugs that say
"I've got you; I understand."

Instead, we're a story
of almosts,
of echoes,
of smiles that don't reach our eyes.

Still, I keep hoping,
Keep wishing,
For a day when "I'm fine"
Turns into "Let me tell you how I really feel."

But deep down,
I know,
It might never happen.
And that's the saddest part,
we're never going to be
the story
I wish we were.

ONE STEP CLOSER

You changed as well, as if my demons were
creeping on you.

I look at you,

We are best friends,

yet, what's left of that?

Walking side by side—

a memory faded.

My laughter no longer reaches you,

yours doesn't seek mine.

Where did the joy go?

We claimed "best friends,"

a title, now feels like a relic.

I thought you were my anchor,

but even anchors can be lifted.

What shifted?

Our banter, once endless,

now silent as forgotten echoes.

Deep talks under starry skies—
vanished,
like they were mere whispers to the universe,
not promises.

We were best friends,
Weren't we?
Or was that just a dream
now too distant to grasp?

Oh...
The realization is cold,
we're not friends anymore.
How?
When?
Why did it escape me?

We're not,
and in that absence,
everything changed.
The silence became too loud,

and my side too empty.

"We're best friends,"
a ghost of a phrase,
haunting the empty halls
of what we're not,
and what changed.

DARPAN

Mom, aren't you supposed to be the softer
one?
Why does it seem that dad's heart, has more
room for me,
than yours?
Aren't you supposed to wrap me in care,
tender as the morning sun's embrace?

Why does he mute his words
at the sight of my trembling hands,
He's silent, yes, but it feels like he's with me.
You, on the other hand, stand stern,
a cold statue, urging me to just
"Get over it"?
Aren't you the mother?
Why does his silence comfort more than
your voice?

33

You command the room —
stop,
be quiet,
let not a single word dare escape in your
presence.
Aren't your ears meant to catch
my fears, my joys, my endless rants?
Instead, they push them away,
as if my words are mere disturbances
in your day.

Aren't mothers supposed to listen?
To soak up the endless words,
The fears, the dreams, the silly things?
But with you, I must stop,
Bite my tongue, and bury my thoughts deep.
You say, "Enough," before I even speak.

Your eyes, sometimes,
Forge darts of disdain,
While he, he averts his gaze,

Maybe in confusion, maybe in pain.
Still, invisibility feels kinder
Than a look laced with disdain.

Aren't mothers supposed to be the
embodiment of love?
Why then, does dad feel like the closer heart,
The gentler soul, the safer haven?
While your love feels like a locked door I
can't open?

Your love, I know,
Might not wear the same skin as mine,
Or speak in tender whispers at night.
It might be in the hard truths you tell,
In the challenges you think I should fight.

But sometimes, mom,
All I need is to be held a little too tight,
To be heard, to be seen,
Not as a soldier ready for battle,

But as your child, lost in between.

Yet you tell me to leave you alone,
Grow up and stop being such a burden.
Aren't you the mother?
Then why,
why does dad's heart seem softer than yours?

DARPAN

I've always been here, haven't I? Then why
are you scared?

Tears stream down every time I see your
face, Mother,
To think of all the hardships, you did
smother.
It cuts my heart into pieces so vast,
Counting them all, the moments you've
passed.

When I dwell on these thoughts, a scream
rises in my throat,
Why? What did you do to wear this heavy
coat?
Why did you think you deserved such a fate,
And burden yourself with all this weight?
Not to mention, above it all,
A daughter like me, so small, so raw.

When memories flood, I want to release

All those muffled cries that never did cease,
From when you first held me close to your
heart,
That moment alone, stands clear and apart.

When I think of how you look at me with
fear,
I want to shout, let my voice pierce your ear,
"No, Mom! Don't hate me, don't push me
away,
Because you're scared that I might sway,
And turn out to mirror your troubled bay."

When these thoughts grip, I wish you knew,
Being like you isn't the curse you construe.
Not as they dictated, not as he made you
believe,
But a blessing, Mom, that I willingly receive.
Maybe I'm not strong, maybe not bold,
But a heart of gold, just like you, I hold.

DARPAN

Why did everything change, when my love
hasn't changed at all?

You don't really like me, I can see,

your eyes no longer sparkle; they question,

they dart,

finding fault in my grown-up heart.

I defend her, yes, always her,

and it twists your face,

like a picture misaligned on a wall—

I remember when I was your all.

When I was small,

your words were my law,

I had no mind of my own;

you were the king; I was your throne.

Now, opinions form my crown,

and they weigh heavy—

on you more than me.

I stand tall, my own entity.

You miss the child, your shadow, your echo,
who danced to your whims, your yes and no.
But that child grew eyes,
grew heart, grew soul,
saw the world through a new window.

I still want to be your favourite,
still long to be the pride in your eyes,
but these wings I've grown,
darken our skies.

Can you see, Father, how I despise
my own shadow—like you, perhaps, at
times?
Now, at least, something binds us tight—
this shared disdain, under the same night.
Yet this common ground where we now
tread,
fills me with sadness, not peace, instead.

DARPAN

We once shared more than glances,

now, even those don't hold.

Once, I was your steadfast,

now, the distance grows too bold.

Because when I was a child,

I was silver—you, the gold.

*I can live with only your love, but can you
love me?*

Sorry, I forgot,

I thought I could be light and breezy,

Live love like any other,

Not just your daughter, steady, easy.

I forgot my lines again,

Not meant for wild loves or late-night talks,

Just meant to make you proud,

Hear you say in crowded rooms,

"That's my star, my girl," your voice so loud.

But Dad, I'm sorry, I forgot the plot,

The guilt is tight around my throat,

It pulls me back before I stray,

To just your daughter, all I am,

In your eyes, day by day.

My only win, to see you proud,

Nothing more can I allow,
Because, remember—I'm not built for love?

Echoes of your expectations,
Guide my steps through silent fears,
I'm just the girl who lives to please,
Remember, I'm not made for tears.

From your script, I accept this role,
Not a lover, just a soul,
Meant to shine in your proud eyes,
Forgive me, I'm not made for skies.

You can't; because all you've ever known is
to leave me behind.

"Grow up! Learn to be on your own!"
You toss the words back over your shoulder,
Leaving echoes that grow colder,
Not noticing how my small world shakes,
Or how my fragile heart breaks.

You always walk away,
Creating distances I cannot sway.
From tender ages to these harder days,
I've learned to navigate your mazes,
Through corridors of silence,
Paved with quiet compliance.

The world outside looms large and fierce,
With shadows lurking, ready to pierce.
Crowded streets, faces blur into night,
Every corner hides a fright.
Yet, there I stand—alone, unguided,

In the chaos, uninvited.

It's strange how I still search for you,
In the faces, the crowds, in the cold morning
dew.
Hoping for a sign, for a change,
A reason not to feel so estranged.
But your lessons in loneliness,
Teach heartache and nothing less.

Each time you leave, it's as if you say,
"Find your way, but alone you must stay."
I'm tethered to a hope that pains me so,
A hope that refuses to let go.
Yet here I am, still waiting, still paused,
In the silence of your lost cause.

Why must I always be the one to learn
The harshness of the world at every turn?
Left behind, not because I'm slow,
But because you choose to let me go.

With every step away you take,
A piece of my spirit, you unknowingly rake.
And in the end, what's left is just me,
Holding on to what could never be.

*And how to make my life something I
despise.*

Birthdays loom,
heavy and unkind—
I dread them,
especially yours, and mine.

Yours, because it brings back the light
we once shared,
dimming now,
shadowed by the distance we barely
acknowledge.

Mine, because it's a reminder,
of laughter turned stale,
of the echo of us clinking glasses,
now silent as the candles flicker and die.

We used to make a day of it,
yours and mine—

splashing brightness, pretending
the sparkles in our eyes were joy
and not the sheen of unshed tears.

Now, there's just the calendar,
flipping its pages with a sigh,
as I cross out dates
that used to mean
more.

"Who celebrates birthdays anyway?" you
scoffed,
voice hollow,
and I laughed—a brittle, jagged sound,
agreeing, because what else could I do?

So, I stopped celebrating,
a quiet surrender of joy,
and you, you stopped wishing,
words withheld that once flowed so easy.

DARPAN

I grew to despise my birthday,
a day marked by the absence
of your voice,
a reminder of how spaces grow
to gulfs between two hearts.

And so,
birthdays became a tally of loss—
me losing my joy for mine,
and you, somehow along the way,
stopped loving me.

Each year, a quiet echo,
a ghost of a party,
where the only thing left to celebrate
is the memory of what used to be,
and the mourning
of what will never
be again.

ONE STEP CLOSER

You know everything, don't you? Yet I'm
unknown to you.

You know the fragility of my heart,
A delicate vase on a high shelf—
You watch as it teeters on the edge,
Unmoved by the impending shatter.

You notice when I crave solitude,
A little room to breathe and stretch—
Yet you open the gates,
Inviting the world to tread across my peace.

You understand my dread of neglect,
The silence that screams in my ears—
Yet you turn your gaze away,
Often and deliberately, blinding yourself to
my form.

You are aware of my unease in crowds,
The way I shrink and fold within—

Yet you push me into the throng,
A lamb amidst the wolves.

You see my reverence for my father,
The pedestal I place him upon—
With a word, a gesture, you tilt my view,
Tarnishing the shine with strokes of doubt.

You know of my good intentions,
How earnestly I strive to please—
Yet your lips craft tales and whispers,
Sowing seeds of disdain where respect once
grew.

You recognize my love for quiet,
The precious pause between chaos—
You choose then to strike the drum,
Filling silence with relentless din.

You acknowledge your love for me,
A fact as firm as earth—

But in moments lost, in days forgotten,
You misplace your heart where I can't find it.

And so, you know—
Yes, you know all too well—
Yet knowing isn't loving,
And seeing isn't saving.
My heart, a thin glass under your watchful
eyes,
Already cracked, readies to break.

DARPAN

I hope me and my words, both stay
unknown forevermore.

I hope these verses escape your view,

And if not, may it blur as you skim through.

You won't read—

your disregard is nothing new.

But if curiosity catches you, just misconstrue.

Dismiss it, as you've dismissed my pain,

But if it haunts you, know it's all in vain.

When have you held my sorrow

or the strain?

Or heard the silence after the rain?

Like forgotten memories in old, dusty

albums,

you won't remember all my champagne

problems.

54

55

Can you look at me

cause I'm

<u>BLUE & GREY</u>

56

One

I used to cry,

now those tears don't fall,

they've turned to red,

a crimson hint in each drop spread.

Yet, no tears slide down my face,

have I drifted from the human race?

Was it more human before,

to weep over the slightest slights,

mourned by none but me,

where every little hurt became a sea?

I keep smiling,

though my heart hurts, I smile still,

At their mean words, cold as a chill,

Their harsh behaviour, a bitter pill,

And their derogatory language, sharp to kill.

Am I not human anymore?

Was I more human before
When I used to fight,
Say "no, you're wrong," take back the night,
"Respect my space," defend my right,
Or when tears flowed, not hidden from
sight?

Was I more human,
When I actually cried tears,
Didn't cry blood,
Or bled tears,
Facing each day with newfound fears?

Two

When you look at me, do you really see,
The trust that broke, so silently?
It used to be easy, like breathing air,
Now it's gone, doesn't seem fair.

They tell me, "Try, just once more,"
But they don't see the closed door.
I trusted once, with all my heart,
Then watched it all, just fall apart.

"She won't hurt you," I thought, believed,
Wasn't ready for the hurt received.
The friend I trusted, who should've cared,
Left me wondering why I dared.

"You can trust her," I told myself,
But her words now sit on a dusty shelf.
What she said, it cut so deep,
Made it hard to sleep, hard to keep.

Sorry might come, from her lips,
But trust, like glass, once cracked, it slips.
It's not about the sorry, or the mend,
It's about the trust, that reached its end.

Why can't I trust? You ask me now,
It's lost, somewhere, somehow.
It's not something you can just get back,
Like trying to fill, what's now a crack.

So, when you ask, look in my eyes,
See the trust that fell, that says goodbye.
It's not easy, can't just pretend,
That's the story, start to end.

Three

"Go speak!"
"If you don't now, you'll forever linger here,
trailing behind everyone."
"You will cry fore—"

Stop.
Halt right there.
Say no more.

Unless you've felt the tremors
That cage my words
And anchor my voice to silence,
Do not urge me to speak.

Unless you've touched the chill on my skin,
Heard my heart racing against time,
Or felt the dread that cloaks my breath,
Stay your advice.

For your words,
though meant to push me forward,
Only remind me of the chains I wear.

Do not command, but listen,
And maybe then, you'll understand
Why my voice, though quiet,
Holds a storm beneath its calm.

Four

Sometimes I wonder why they still see a
child in me—
I've walked alone longer than they know.
Why then am I still called a kid?
And if I am a child,
Why is it that I feel I've seen it all?

They urge me to conform,
To become a pleasing fiction,
A beautiful lie, not truly myself.
But if they never cherished who I was,
Unremarkable and raw,
Why do they seek to shape me now?

Long have I navigated my path alone;
Still, they label me a child.
If that's so...
Why can't they let me cherish childhood?
Why clip my wings,

Dismantle my name,
And sow seeds of fear about the world
outside?

Five

Are you acquainted with who I am, truly so?
If not, have you tried, or is it just for show?
Do you know the hue I hold dear,
The things that draw from my eyes a tear,
Or the shade with which I paint my sky's
glow?

Do you comprehend me in any real way,
Beyond the mere name you casually say?
Are you aware of my favourite ice cream
taste,
Or that I relish the role of a silent, watchful
wraith?

Do you sense the sadness cloaked in today?
It marks another year; it's my birthday.
Yet, what's sadder still, if truth be told,
Is that this day, too, you've overlooked, left
out in the cold.

Do you see, then, why my heart feels tight?
Why shadows loom larger than the light?
It's not just that you've forgotten the date,
But that your absence in these moments feels
like fate.

Six

I miss them,
left them behind, I know,
a decision I made,
one that haunts me.
It's all my fault.

If they were here,
they'd never make me a joke,
never let me feel
this hollow, empty ache.

I miss the chats,
the crush talks,
the nonsense jokes,
our laughter filling the void
like light in a darkened room.

Above all, I miss them.
I miss having friends,

the comfort of knowing
someone all too well.
I miss crying over champagne problems,
pretending they were the end of the world,
when really, they were just
tiny cracks in our lives.

It's my fault, I know.
I could've stayed,
could've walked with them,
could've held on tighter,
could've whispered
the truths I kept hidden.

But I didn't.
I walked away,
chose silence over words,
chose distance over closeness.

Now my life is a lonely place,
a barren room

echoing with what-ifs and could-have-beens.

I built these walls so high,

no one can climb them,

no one can stay.

I watch the world from behind glass,

a silent observer,

remembering the warmth of their presence,

the way they understood

my unspoken thoughts.

But now,

there's only cold,

only solitude,

a self-imposed exile

from the love I once knew.

Seven

Each morning dims a piece of me—
I step on the cold scale
and it tells me if today
I deserve to eat.

Sometimes I trick myself,
believing things are looking up,
but that's just a shadow,
not the truth.

I face the mirror,
a stranger stares back,
and I turn away.

I turn away,
losing a bit more of myself
with every glance that doesn't recognize
the person I used to be.

DARPAN

The days blend together,
each one a monochrome melody
of rituals that leave me hollow.
I count each bite like a miser counts coins,
saving up for a salvation
that never comes.

Friends speak, their words floating
like leaves I can't quite catch.
They say I'm getting better,
their smiles trying to stitch
a quilt of normalcy around me.

But their eyes miss
the silent screams and the nightly battles
where shadows choke my dreams.
Every "It's okay" they utter
is another mile in the maze
of my quiet despair.

The sun sets again,

and I am no closer to peace than before.
Underneath the starlit void,
I wonder if the sky is as empty as I feel,
or if it too is hiding its face,
ashamed of what it cannot heal.

The night deepens, and so does the ache,
an echo in the cavity of my ribcage
where a heart once beat without fear.
Tomorrow looms—a promise, a threat—
and I know,
I will lose myself a little more.

Eight

Here we stand, you and I,

in a room where silence has weight,

and I'm fading, slowly, right before you.

I tell you I'm scared,

but it seems like just whispers in the wind to

you.

Colors around me turn to shadows,

blues and greys meld into a storm,

you say it's nothing—

yet it feels like everything is crumbling.

My voice raises in desperation,

echoing around us, sharp and scared,

you're still, calm, unaffected,

as if my fears are just echoes, not screams.

Why can't you see?

The ground is slipping beneath me,

I'm calling out to you, reaching,
but you're just out of touch, out of reach.

This isn't just a phase,
it's not the passing clouds or a dimming
light,
it's the dark swallowing me whole,
while you stand there, not even flinching.

We're here together, yet I'm alone,
wrapped in my own cold fears,
I tell you I'm losing myself,
and you, you don't even blink.
How can you not feel this chill?
Am I invisible, am I so easily ignored?
I need you to see me, really see me,
before I fade away, before I'm nothing at all.

Nine

In the quiet unspooling of day into night,

I sit with the numbness,

my constant companion,

a silent partner at the breakfast table

where the toast burns slightly,

and the coffee tastes like shadows.

It accompanies me on the drive to nowhere,

where red lights bleed into each other,

blurring into a monochrome of stop and go,

and I realize, I've forgotten the destination

that once felt so important.

It's there in the small talk,

a buffer between me and the world,

words float like icebergs in a dead sea,

only their tips touching air,

while the bulk of what's unsaid,

what's unfelt,

remains submerged and hidden.

We dine on apathy,
a flavourless meal that fills the belly,
but never nourishes.
It holds my hand tighter than any lover,
a grip so familiar, so cold,
it must be love,
or something like it.

At night, it tucks me in,
a blanket woven from the softest threads of
grey.
We lay in bed, staring at the ceiling
as if it were the sky,
as if it could show us stars,
but there are none.

It whispers, "Sleep, now."
And I obey,
falling into a dreamless sleep,

where even dreams dare not linger.

In this partnership,
I've misplaced the meaning of 'alone,'
for numbness fills every corner,
every crevice,
until I am full,
overflowing with the void.

Tomorrow, it promises more of the same,
and I find solace in the promise,
because feeling nothing
isn't as painful as feeling everything.

And so we go on,
numbness and I,
a perfect match,
until the end,
when even the sadness fails to touch,
and the heart forgets how to ache.

Ten

How much sadness did you think I had in
me,
For so many tragedies?

Did you imagine
that my heart
could stretch endlessly
to contain all this sorrow,
that my soul was a vessel
for every drop of grief
this life could pour?

You looked at me,
eyes full of assumptions,
never seeing the fractures
hidden beneath my surface,
the hairline cracks
spreading like a spider's web,
ready to shatter

at the next whispered heartbreak.

How much sad did you think I had,
to give,
to bear,
to live through?

Every tear a testament
to resilience,
every sigh
a quiet rebellion
against the weight
pressing down,
crushing,
but never quite breaking.

How much sadness did you think
a person could hold
before they become sadness itself,
a walking elegy,
a living epitaph,

for all the loves and friendships lost,
for all the dreams left behind?

You saw strength,
but mistook it for an endless reservoir,
not realizing
that even the deepest wells
can run dry,
that even the strongest walls
can crumble,
under the relentless tide
of too many tragedies.

Eleven

Loving you feels like drowning,
in murky waters where hope cannot breathe.
Each inhale a gulp of cold despair,
your indifference a tide pulling me under.

My feet can't touch the ground,
flailing in the dark, seeking something solid
but grasping only the liquid chill of your
retreat.
Each promise unkept floats past me,
buoyant with the irony of their emptiness.

Deeper into the depths,
where light fears to linger,
the pressure of your silence crushes my
chest.
I reach for you, my hands sweeping through
cold nothing,
while my heart beats slower,

weakened by the effort of unreciprocated
love.

There is no dramatic rescue,
no hand to pull me from these depths,
just the slow cessation of struggle,
a quiet acquiescence to the inevitable.

Here in the depths of my despair,
your absence is a weight heavier than the
sea,
and I am left alone,
drowned in the silent aftermath of loving
you.

In the end, it is not water, but sorrow that
fills my lungs.
The realization that I am alone
here in the deep, with your shadow on the
surface—
a distant, uncaring sun.

Twelve

"But you never said you loved me..."

Wasn't letting you go the loudest declaration
of all?
Watching you smile beside him,
While my dreams silently fell apart?
Seeing him give you everything he has,
While my love sits quietly, isolated in my
heart?
Did I need to voice it out aloud?
When my every action screamed so
fervently?
Did it need to be spoken,
When everyone around us could see, know it
all,
Except you... too absorbed in him to notice
The one who loved you, unnoticed and
unchosen.

Thirteen

Do you ever wonder,
How empty I must be of myself
To be so filled with you?

How much of me remains, I wonder,
When so much of what I was
Has been emptied to make room for you?

Now, with each day that passes,
I feel the echoes of who I used to be,
Drowning in the shadow of your presence.

What is left of my own thoughts,
My own dreams, my own desires,
When they are all replaced by fragments of
you?

I search for traces of the person I once knew,
Lost somewhere between your smile

And the silence that follows.

85

Perhaps, in the end, there is nothing left,
Just an empty vessel
Where you once dwelled.

Fourteen

You swore that you loved me, but where
were the clues
when tears stained my cheeks and my heart
was bruised?
You spoke of forever, a future so bright,
Yet in my darkest hours, you vanished from
sight.

Promises whispered like leaves in the breeze,
Fleeting and fickle, too easy to seize.
I clung to each word, a desperate creed,
But words are just air; they're not what I
need.

In the silence that followed, my doubts took
your place,
Each one a reminder of a looming disgrace.
How could love's fire reduce to cold ash?

Gone without trace, I became a forgotten
flash.

Alone in the shadows, I puzzled through
pain,
Replaying the moments again and again.
Yet amidst the echoes of our shattered
dream,
I found my resolve, or so it would seem.

I stood at the altar, draped in white hue,
The crowd blurred in vision, but there was
no you.
A promise of always, empty and stark—
A church full of people, but I was in the
dark.

I realized then, as I stood there so blue,
That waiting for you was futile to pursue.
The vows unspoken, the kiss left undone,
I walked away slowly; I knew you had won.

Yet victory's taste was bitter and cruel,
For you lost as well, oh pitiful fool.
You swore that you loved me, but gave no
real proof,
And I died on the altar, waiting for you.

Fifteen

Would I ever be enough?
I've set aside the pen you despise,
Abandoned dreams in a quiet sigh,
My very breath—a compromise.
Yet still, I fall short in your eyes.
You never voice the stark truth—
What does it mean
To be enough?

I've molded my voice to softer tones,
Erased my footsteps from paths once
roamed,
Dimmed my light until it barely shone.
Still, the distance between us only grows.
Your silence, a void cold and rough,
Leaves me wondering—
What is enough?

Through years draped in silent yearning,

I've sought the love for which I'm burning.

Yet your approval remains a door unturning,

Each withheld word a quiet spurning.

So here I stand, weary and scuffed,

Still asking at the dusk of trust

—Would I ever be enough?

Sixteen

Suffocation isn't enough to kill me.
But words are.
They sink deeper, burrowing,
echoes in a hollow room.

They fracture the soul,
leaving splinters that ache,
long after the voices have faded.

Whispers that cling like shadows,
draining color from the world,
each letter a blade,
carving wounds invisible, yet unhealing.

Silent screams, unheard cries,
a heart bruised and tender.
No air can heal what silence breaks.
In the end, it's the words
that leave me breathless.

Suffocation might take my breath,
but words take everything else.
They hollow me out,
piece by piece,
until there's nothing left to take,
nothing left to break.

Seventeen

Hating myself comes as naturally as
breathing now,
a reflex, nothing more,
born from the many nights spent replaying
old conversations
like scratched records that never find their
resolve.
Each moment, each memory, a fragment,
piercing through what little peace I gather.

The world moves, relentless and unyielding,
and I watch, unseen,
from behind the smeared glass of my own
isolation.
Where smiles once flickered, a vacancy
reigns,
and I'm left crafting apologies from the
silence

that stretches between the words I can no
longer summon.

My days bleed into each other—
indistinguishable, grey—
marked only by the steady cadence of a heart
that beats,
but doesn't feel.
The mirror reflects a stranger's tired gaze,
eyes that flicker with the dull sheen of
unshed tears,
a soul too tired to weep, too broken to
mend.

In the quiet corners of evening's embrace,
where shadows are the deepest,
my thoughts turn against me—
sharp and cruel,
a swarm of wasps in the dying light.
I am the keeper of old scars,
the silent battleground of lost wars.

Every step is a betrayal,

every smile a mask that slips—

revealing the fractures,

the deep, dark crevices of a mind shadowed

by doubts.

Friends speak, but their words are just

echoes

from a life I once thought I could live.

Time, they say, heals all wounds,

but mine are stubborn things;

they cling like ivy,

wrapping their thorny vines tight around my

limbs,

holding me captive in a garden of thorns.

The moon is a silent witness to my

unraveling,

casting a pale light on pages filled with

words

that bleed right through.
Each sentence a sigh, each paragraph a
plea—
the unfinished letters of a soul too weary to
fight.

So, I write this now, a testament, not of
hope,
but of surrender,
to the endless night that awaits.
Each word a stone in the heavy pocket of my
despair,
sinking me deeper into the murky waters of
forgetfulness.
This is not a cry for salvation,
nor a search for light.
This is a letter to
—the nothing I've become.

Eighteen

I'm always sad,
Sad to the point it seems all that remains
Is just an endless echo of melancholy.
You notice the shadow that lingers over my
smile,
But do you really see me?

With every tear that escapes,
Every forced grin that fades,
Do you really look at me?
Understand the hues that tinge my soul,
Colors deeper than just blue and grey.

And as I stand here,
Wrapped in my own shivering silhouette,
Can you love the quiet despair,
Embrace the storm that roars in the silence
of my heart?

Will you hold me close,
Even when my laughter has fallen away,
And all that's left is the cold, numb grey of
dusk?
Because here I am—
Wondering if you can love me,
If you can stay
When I'm blue and grey.

Take me to

THE LAKES

where all the poets

went to die.

ONE STEP CLOSER

The summer never turned pretty

What if, instead of the quiet solitude of my
room all summer,
I laughed with friends, like scenes from
vibrant dramas?
Where every day unfurled in a burst of
sunlight, secrets to share,
and we lived in a rush of ice cream runs,
under stars we'd compare.

Maybe we'd sprawl across sunlit fields, wide,
daisy chains adorning hair, tied,
voices weaving through the air—lively,
uncontained,
Or dance through the city's heartbeat,
pulse racing
with the thrill of being young, sustained.

We could have chased the fading light from
sunset to night's embrace,

not a moment lost in the chase,
each laugh a bright note in the warm
summer's pace.

But as the golden glow fades into cooler
whispers of fall,
reality settles like dust, filling the empty hall.
The laughter fades to a hush,
the fields lie still, the city's pulse calms to a
mush,
and the vibrant throng of friends dissolves—
for they were but shadows in my longing's
pulse.

And here, in the quiet aftermath of what
never came to be,
I sit alone, silently.
The summer never turned pretty,
it remained just a series of grey days and
wishful dreams, gritty,

while I waited, alone, for a season that never
truly arrived, pity.

Found a family that never found me

I hate the way you interrupt,
Cutting my words before they're free.
And how swiftly your gaze shifts—
From the world to where I be,
Once you're done with your story.

I hate how small you make me feel,
Diminished, lost within my skin,
Questioning everything I thought I knew.
And the lies you tell about love,
As if they don't leave marks, harsh and true.

But most of all,
I hate—
I hate that my heart won't hate you,
Not even slight,
Because through everything, you are my
light.

You're the colors with which I paint my sky,
my chosen shade of blue.
You're a family that I found,
Family that didn't quite seek me around.

I hate that I'm just another in the crew,
Never the special, never the few.
Yet, I cherish that I chose you in the love
lane,
My unintentional, yet destined plan.

It's the paradox of you—
The comfort that wounds deep,
The presence that suffocates, so rife.
And as I stand on the edge of our shared
dreams,
I wonder if the love I feel
Is merely the echo of my own strife,
Calling back to me across the void, serene.
And it breaks me—
That the biggest lie might not be from you,

But the one I tell myself each night,
That this, us, can ever be right.

Always the stain, never the stained

I wear scars like verses,
inked in someone else's crimson.
Misery etched upon the parchment of my
skin,
not by my own hand, but thrust upon me
by those who see not the ruin they wreak.

Each morning I wake,
a battlefield,
where I alone am left to mourn the dead—
the death of dreams, of quiet joys.
Their accusations, sharp and swift,
claim me the culprit in my own demise,
yet I was but a canvas
for their crimson deeds.

I've become an echo
in the chambers of the falsely accused,
where truth is bent and twisted

like the limbs of tortured willows.
They painted my soul with shadows,
claimed sanctuary in their falsehoods,
left me a husk, hollow and wanting.

Now, here I lie, a specter of verses,
haunting the edges of my own life,
watching the world with weary eyes,
tarnished, tainted—
always the stain, never the stained.

Why must I carry this weight,
this relentless reminder of sins not mine?
A poet, meant to craft beauty from pain,
yet I forge chains from these heavy, leaden
lines.

And so, I fade—a whisper on the wind,
a footnote in the anthologies of anguish,
forgotten, forlorn,

forever the bearer of another's bloodied
legacy.

Only tears remain

My boredom is bone-deep, and my hobbies
quietly drift away,
like fragments of my peace of mind.
Tears fall, unbidden,
as the grey sky weeps with me,
its tears melding with mine
in a silent symphony of sorrow.
The days stretch, long and empty,
each moment longer than the last,
each heartbeat a heavy thud
in a chest filled with echoes.

I whisper to the shadows,
but they do not whisper back,
only lengthening
as the light fades,
leaving me alone
with the quiet dread
that tomorrow

will be just as hollow.

Memory of your love

Do I have a good memory?
I'm unsure, for all I recall is joy,
Yet my melancholy was infectious.
I remember your absence,
More than your presence—
But do I have a good memory?
I seem to have misplaced my feelings,
The tears that shaped my tender years,
And the endless babble that branded me
garrulous.
My crafty pranks that earned me labels of
'cunning' and 'sly,'
Yet it's the echo of your voice,
Calling me those names, that still draws
tears.
Do I have a good memory?
I think not,
For the memory of your love,
Seems more illusion than truth.

Fear of the thoughts

Once the fear was a shadow in the dark,
A whisper in the hallway, an unexpected spark.
But now, it's a tide that rises with each thought,
A deeper, darker sea where my peace is caught.

The old fears, ghosts and specters in the night,
Seem gentler now, less capable of fright.
It's the thoughts that spin, relentless in my head,
That brings the true terror, the deepest dread.

No haunted house, no creaking midnight floor,

Scares me as much as the thoughts I can't ignore.
It's the whispering doubts, the endless inner cries,
That holds more horror than a ghost's surprise.

I flee from the fears no door can keep out,
The fears that follow fill me with doubt.
Running from the echoes inside my own mind,
From the demons that whisper, "You'll never find..."

I dodge every reflection, afraid of what I'll see—
Not a monster, but my own eyes staring back at me.
In the mirror, a shadow, the darkest part of my soul,

The part that's broken, that will never be
whole.

And so I run, but the running never ends,
From the fears that break, from what never
mends.
Running into the night, where the dark is
deep,
From the thoughts that haunt me even in my
sleep.

For now, the greatest fear, the hardest to
evade,
Is not of ghosts or darkness or the sharp
edge of a blade.
It's the fear of knowing this is how it will
always be,
Me, running forever from these harsh
thoughts,
trying to flee.

Haunted

I'm in a daze, every second, every day,
And each time the voices in my head, they
play.
Like an unstoppable turmoil, deep and vile,
Pulling me down into the dark soil.

I cry and cry, still waiting for a sign,
Something to feel alive, not just in line.
I try to muffle sobs, keep my thoughts from
you,
But it's hard to contain, I pretend I'm fine—
what else to do?
Because what if your thoughts of me mirror
my own?
What if you deem me as not someone dear,
but someone you'd disown?

I want to show you every side of mine,

But fear it will not make your heart more
kind.
I try so hard to prove I'm not what's wrong,
And that every corner of this house indeed
prolongs my mournful song.

How can I trust when you say I belong,
When inside I'm the one I've loathed so
long?
How can you claim your positive view
Will satisfy a soul so twisted,
When everything in this world feels nothing
but haunted?

Love that never evolved

He walks through life, his heart untouched
by scars above,
His eyes never blurred by the tears of lost
love.
People fall like leaves around him,
charmed by his smile so fine—
He can't grasp what draws them near,
Nor what binds them to his heart's distant
line.

She holds her love like a cup overflowing,
ready to share with any wind that's blowing.
Yet her warmth escapes, slipping cracks
unseen,
finding no steady hands to hold,
not knowing how to give without losing
what's been.

They walk their paths, like lines that never
meet—
he, untouched by love's deep heat,
she, drowning in its flood without retreat.
Their paths cross, a brief eclipse in time,
her too much, his too little—neither in
rhyme.

They part as stars, misaligned in their tracks;
She's drained, a well run dry, from giving too
much, too lax,
He walks on, still baffled by love's syntax,
Feels its ghost around, vague as wax,
Ever haunting, elusive, slipping through the
cracks.

I lost my mind over you

"You never loved me."

Never loved you?
Maybe, because love is just a word,
too simple to encapsulate
the immensity of my emotions.
It was beyond that,
beyond the common beats of hearts,
deeper than the soul's quiet whispers in the
dark.

It was a universe expanding,
wild and unrestrained—
so vast, I lost myself
within its boundless skies.
I became a star flung far from its galaxy,
Adrift in the space where only your memory
resides.

DARPAN

Tonight, the stars refuse to shine,
as if even they know of my despair.
The sky, a vast expanse of darkness,
mirrors the emptiness within me.

I sit by the window,
where shadows stretch long
across the floor, whispering secrets
only the lonely can understand.

Your absence is a void,
a black hole consuming
the light of my life.
Memories of you flicker
like distant galaxies,
too far away to touch.

In the silence, I hear your voice,
a faint echo that haunts

the corridors of my mind.
Each word, a reminder
of promises unkept,
of love that slipped
through the cracks of our hands.

The night is heavy,
laden with the weight of all
that we lost, and all
we could never be.
I reach out into the darkness,
but there is nothing to hold,
nothing to grasp
except the cold air and the ache
of knowing you are gone.

Tonight, the stars refuse to shine,
and I wonder if they mourn with me,
if they, too, feel the sting
of a love that has died.
I close my eyes and let

the darkness consume me,
hoping that sleep will bring
a temporary reprieve
from this endless night.

All you saw was the blood I bled

Why did you see only my blood upon you?
How did you miss the tears in my eyes,
That I poured out my heart, my truth,
Emptied my soul, cut all my ties?
You gazed at me, eyes unseeing,
As I gave everything, gave all,
Every ounce of life, of being,
To fill the emptiness, the void so tall.

But all you saw was the blood I bled,
The stains it left, the crimson tide.
That's all you remember, the words unsaid,
The memories lost, the love denied.
You forget I gave all of myself,
Just to fill the void within your heart.
And when it was filled, no longer an elf,
You hollowed me out, tore me apart.

Left me an empty shell, made me bleed,

And as I bled, I knew, it was clear,
There was nothing you felt, no love, no
need,
Not even pity, nothing dear.
You took my all, left me in ruin,
Turned my heart so cold, so cruel, so
inhuman,
And never once looked back at me,
Not even a glance, not one repent.

Failure, but still me

The room's empty now
but if you listen close—
the walls chuckle softly
I don't know if it's on my pain
or my attempts that went in vain
but it mocks me, "oh, you'll never be..."
and I know, so I stay silent
'cause nothing can change this prophecy
it laughs out loud, the voice a contagious
nightmare
I can't help but cloud all the thoughts never
held dear
but it laughs and it laughs, screaming—
"you're nothing but a failure" it's bitter
words
Oh, good is it scheming?
I get up and wipe the tears
"a failure but this is me, and I will never
change I fear."

The lakes

Take me to the lakes where all the poets
went to die I don't belong
Windermere's peaks loom, a somber place to
cry
I'm setting off, but not alone—
My muse clings tight, steeped in blues.
With shades drawn, pages fluttering like
heartbeats,
I don't belong here
Under sullen skies, I long for waters deep
where whispered echoes sink in silent sighs.

Lead me where ink bleeds quietly into
weeping streams
where words dissolve under the weight of
dreams.
By the lakeside, where sorrow sleeps,
Let me drift—
a fading verse on the lips of the breeze.

Yes, take me to the lakes where all the poets
went to lie
where their echoes end and even verses die.
There, I'll lay my pen down, beneath the
shroud of grey,
to trace their steps into the still, eternal bay.

DARPAN

129

<u>WHO'S AFRAID OF LITTLE OLD ME</u>

(darpan's version)

In my quietest moments,
the whispers begin—
not the soft murmurs of a curious mind,
but hissing, spitting malcontents aligned
that fill the well of my chest
with stone, pressed.

They say, "Smile, why don't you?"
as though my lips are stubborn doors anew
welded shut by rust,
and happiness a guest, just
turned away too often,
now unwilling to soften.

But who sees the effort behind the curvature
of a 'just fine' smile, pure?
A performance perfected in the mirror, dear,

nightly,
under the harsh critique of fluorescent bulbs,
slightly.

I am the master of disguise;
the girl with laugh lines, wise
not fault lines, binds.
My eyes might shine at your jokes,
sparkle at your tales by strokes,
but they are mirrors too—
reflecting only what you want to view.

Beneath, there is an echo chamber solemn
where your voices never reach, fallen.
Echoes of 'should' and 'could',
'more' and 'else', should
they ricochet,
crumbling the pillars of my resolve, they say.

The world spins,
and I spin with it, skins

dizzy,
always on the brink, busy
of tumbling into the abyss
where shadows swallow shadows whole,
amiss.

No,
I am not the girl you know;
I am a ghost in her shell, an echo,
haunting her bones,
whispering of freedom in monotones
in a language forgotten.

The iron taste of silence
is my sacrament, reliance,
my confession
written in the invisible ink of depression
of tears not cried.

And yet, you see none of this.
No, you see none of it, at all.

DARPAN

<u>I WOULD CHOOSE A BEAR OVER A MAN</u>

I would choose a bear over a man
because if a bear hurt me
the world wouldn't question
what I wore,
how I laughed,
or the hour of the night
when my screams echoed through the pines.

I would choose a bear over a man
because his claws, though sharp and
unforgiving,
know nothing of malice;
just hunger, just survival—
not cruelty, not pleasure.
And if blood were drawn,
it would be nature's doing,
not a punishment meted out
with a smirk and a gavel.

ONE STEP CLOSER

I would choose a bear over a man
because after the mauling,
after my last breath fogged the cold air,
he would amble away,
leaving my bones untouched by blame,
my memory free of whispered accusations
and the crushing weight of disbelief.

In the forest, where shadows hold dominion
and the river weeps with the widowed doe,
there, my spirit would rest in the hush,
not haunted by the eyes of those
who judge the tilt of a skirt
or the promise they presume it made.

So, I would choose a bear over a man
because the bear does not feign love
before he strikes.
His nature is clear, laid bare in tooth and
claw—
pure, raw, without deceit.

When he leaves, he leaves nothing but
silence,
not the wreckage of broken promises
or the echo of a love that never was.

I would choose a bear over a man,
because while both might leave me broken,
only one does so without malice—
his departure is simple,
leaving only the quiet rustle of leaves
and no cruel whispers to echo
through the aching woods.

ONE STEP CLOSER

<u>I CAN DO IT WITH A BROKEN HEART</u>

(darpan's version)

I wear my skin like a costume,
draped in illusions of beauty, my bloom.
That shimmer like broken glass in vain,
cutting deep as I smile through the pain.

Enter the hallways of academics,
the race is relentless, so systemic.
A marathon with no end,
where every step is measured to fend,
every breath a struggle against,
the weight of expectations incensed.

There's a quiet war at home,
echoes of disapproval in every dome.
My dreams crumbling, torn apart,
under the pressure of practicality's art,
the poet in me buried alive,
under the debris of "what's right."

The ink dries in my pen,

words trapped in my throat again.

Silenced by the fear of failure's haunt,

the ghost of support,

haunting my every thought,

my dreams slipping away,

like sand through clenched fists, they sway.

But I've learned the art of pretense,

to laugh when my heart is breaking, so

dense.

To shine in the dark,

to fake it until the ache departs,

becomes just another rhythm, not far,

in the symphony of survival, a star.

I'm a master of masks,

a performer on the stage of life,

dancing to the beat of despair,

yet I keep moving, keep hoping,

even as my soul fractures, and sparks,
So I grin like I'm winning, hitting the mark,
'cause I can do it with a broken heart.

DARPAN

139

ONE STEP CLOSER

<u>ONE STEP CLOSER</u>

to death.

I live in the quiet world of words,

Each poem a whisper seldom heard.

With every line I write,

My breath grows light,

Life spills out onto the page,

My heart beats with a softer rage.

"You're lost in your lines."

Yes, this world of words is mine.

So what if I lose myself with every word I

type,

And what if each poem I write

Is a step closer to death?

And what if all I need is you

To bring me back to breath?

ONE STEP CLOSER

DARPAN

<u>ONE STEP CLOSER</u>

(your version)

ABOUT THE AUTHOR

Darpan is a young poet from Delhi, India, currently in her last year of high school. "One Step Closer" is her first book, a collection of poems that dive deep into the world of sadness.

She started writing when she was just 12 years old and hasn't stopped since. For Darpan, writing and literature are a safe haven, a place where she can express emotions that are hard to put into words.

Growing up in Delhi, Darpan has always found inspiration in the bustling city around her, as well as in the quiet moments of reflection. She enjoys crocheting and listening to music, two hobbies that help her unwind and keep her creativity flowing. Whether she's crafting a new piece or getting lost in a song, these activities provide a balance to her writing life.

"One Step Closer" represents a significant milestone for the poet. It's a journey through her innermost thoughts and feelings, shared with the hope that readers will find comfort and connection in her words. She believes that poetry has the power to bridge gaps and bring people closer, one verse at a time.

This book is more than just a collection of poems; it's a piece of her heart, offered to the world. Through her writing, the poet aims to touch the lives of others and offer a sense of solace to anyone who reads her work.

For Information, Contact:
Instagram — https://www.instagram.com/awrtsblue
Email — writerjaek@gmail.com